A-Maze-ing Cool Cars

Tony and Tony Tallarico

kidsbooks Incorporated

Copyright © 2002 Kidsbooks, Inc.
230 Fifth Ave.
New York, NY 10001

Manufactured in Canada

Bugatti EB Veyron

BMW Z8

1933 Dusenberg SJ Speedster

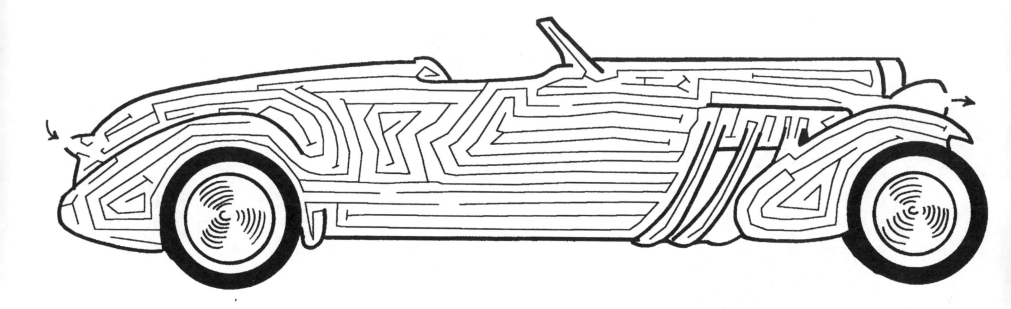

Lexus SC 430

Ford GTO

Ford SVT Mustang CR

Semi Monster wheels

Toyota Spyder

Honda Insight

Chrysler Lightning

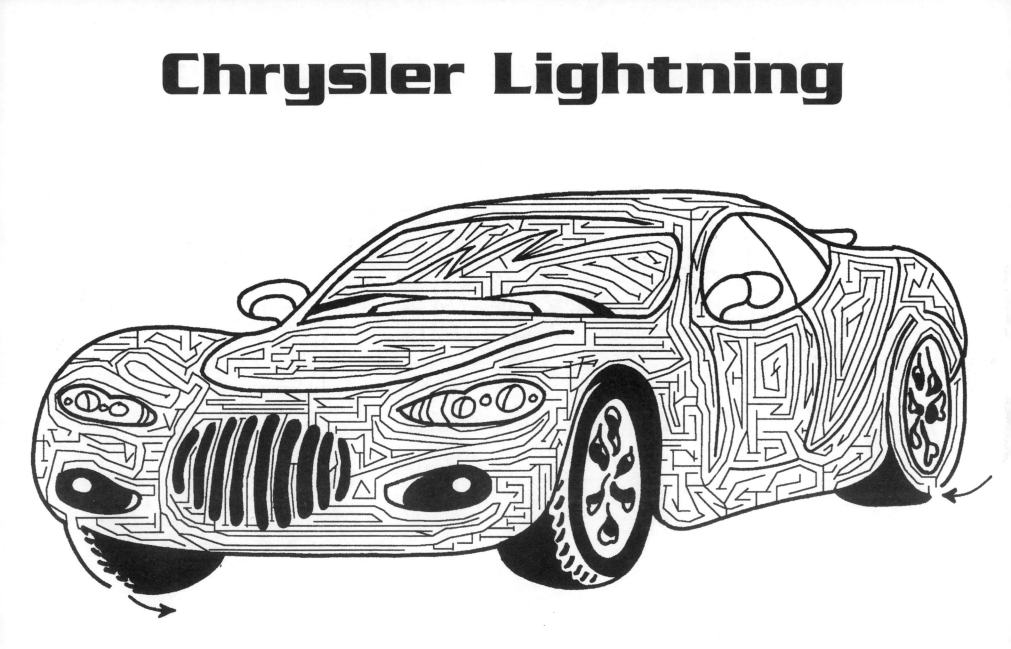

AM General Hummer

1957 Chevrolet Corvette SS Racer

Audi TT

1958 Cadillac
Model 62

Chevrolet Avalanche
Ultimate Utility Vehicle

Ferrari Spider

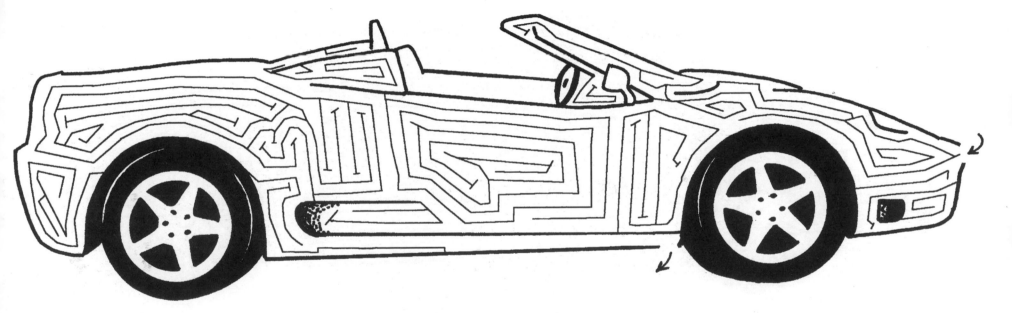

Buick La Crosse

Aluma Coupe

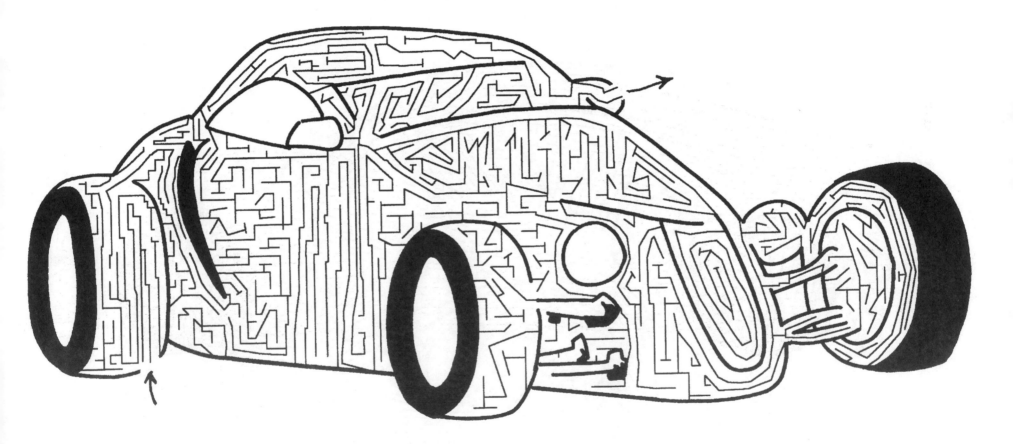

2000 Volkswagon Beetle

Suburu ST-X

Jaguar F Type Concept Car

1961 Chevrolet Corvette

Porsche Pan American

Toyota Celica

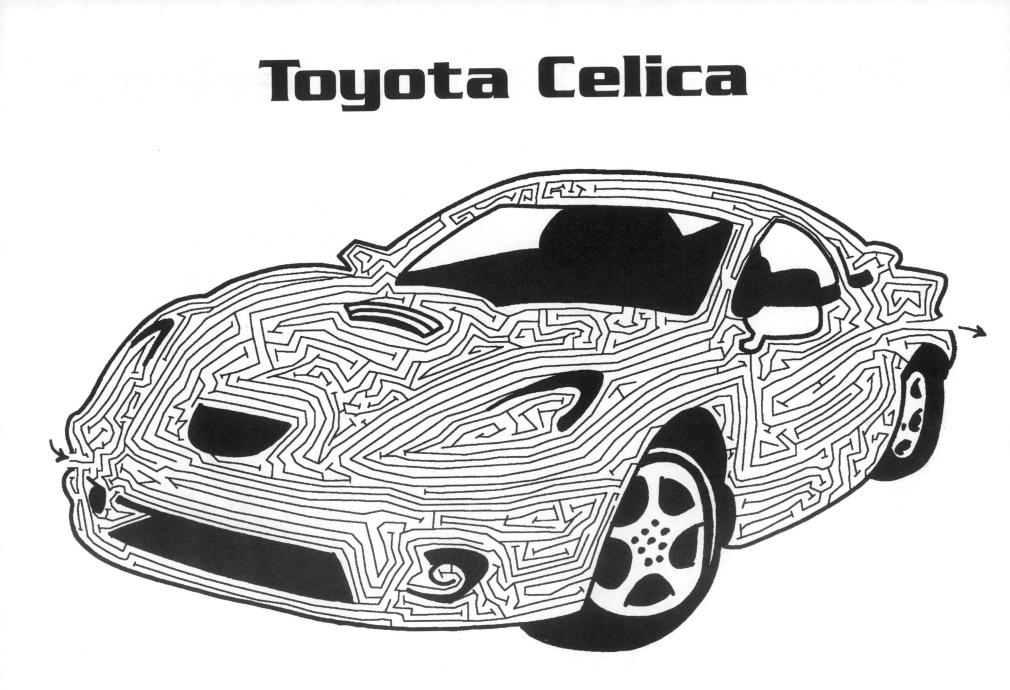

Stock Car Racer

Isuzu Kai

Vector W8
Twin Turbo

Plymouth Prowler

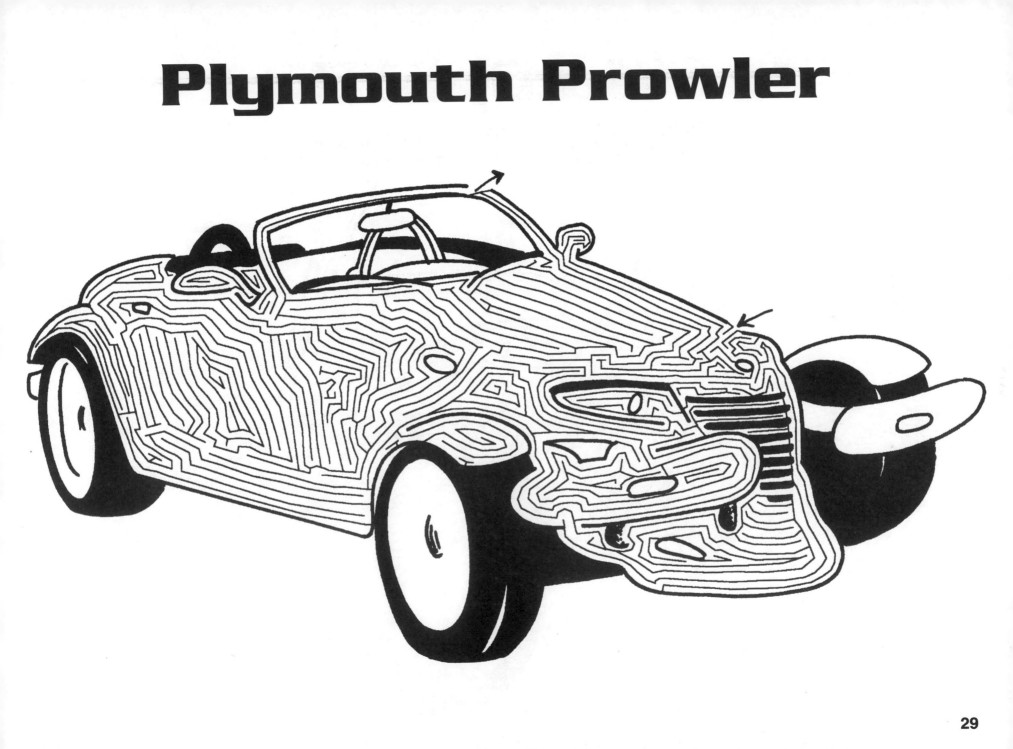

Honda Sprocket

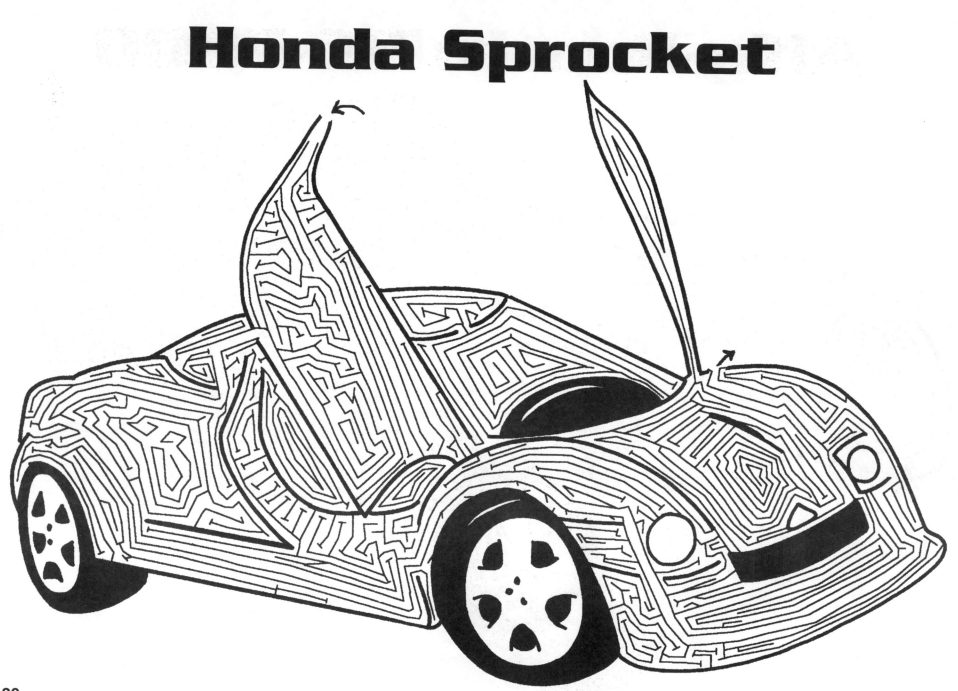

Alfa-Romeo 8C-2900

BMW Sport Wagon

Ford 2001 CrewZer

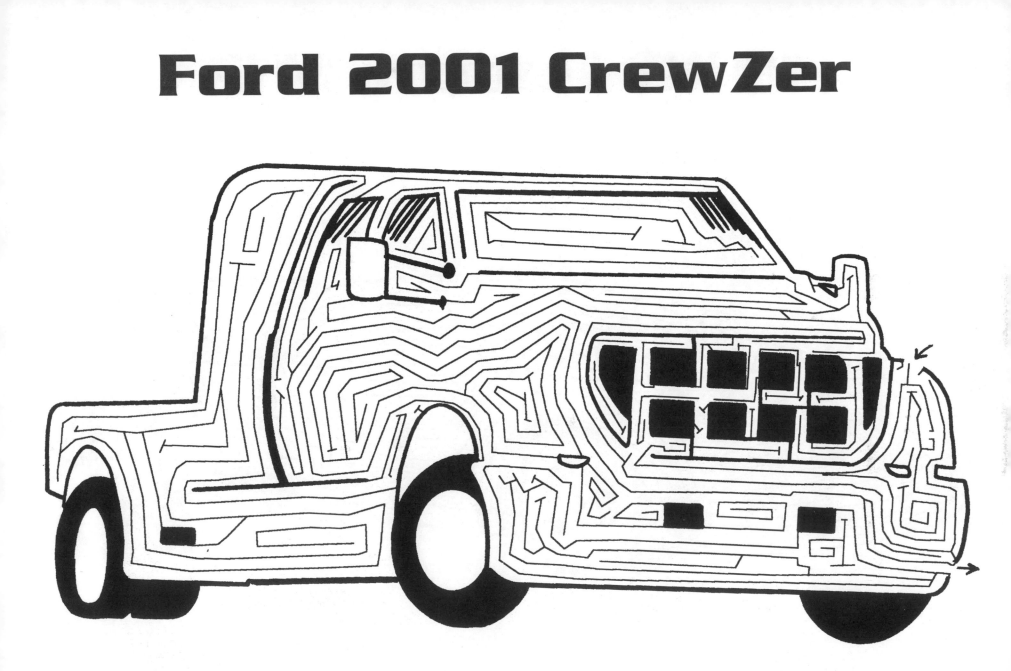

1996 Vector M12

Jeep

Koenig Porsche

Lotus Esprit

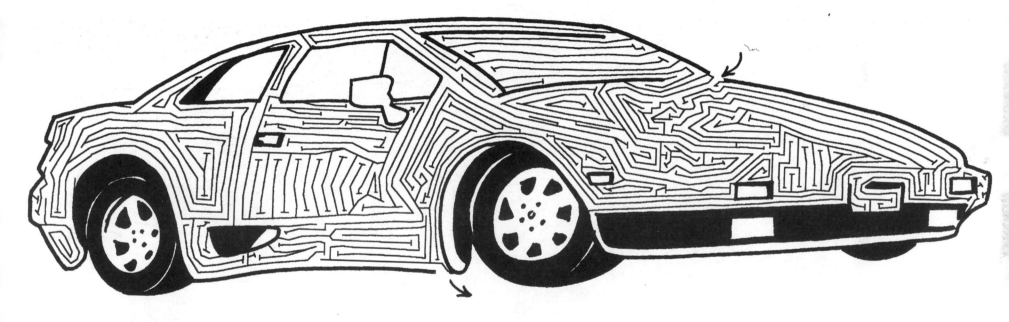

Super SUV

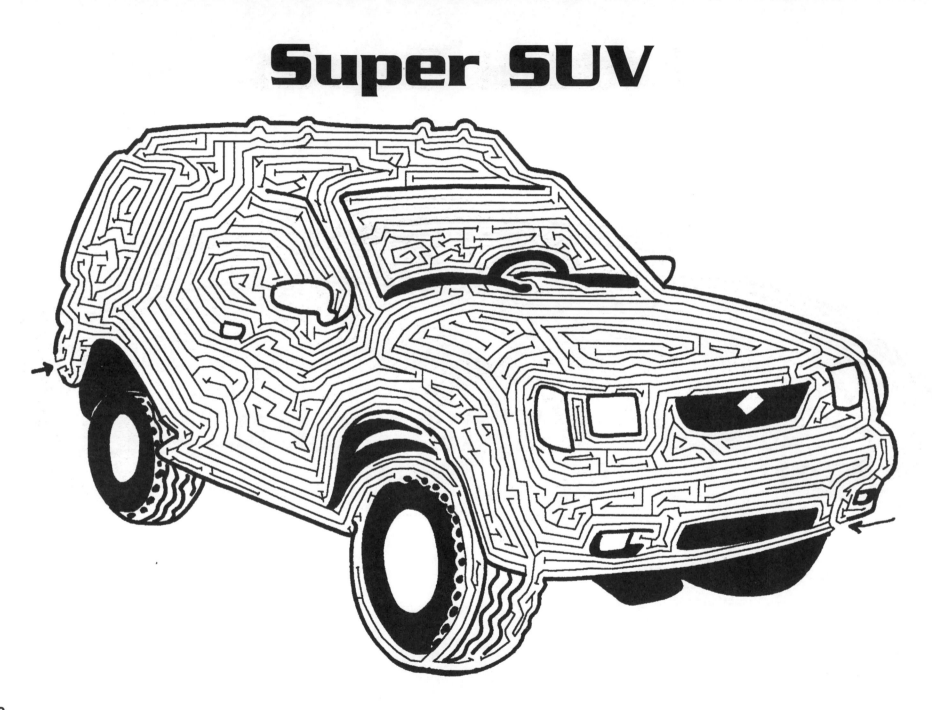

1998 Stola

1952 Lotus MK 111B

Aston Martin DBM Vantage

Porsche Speedster

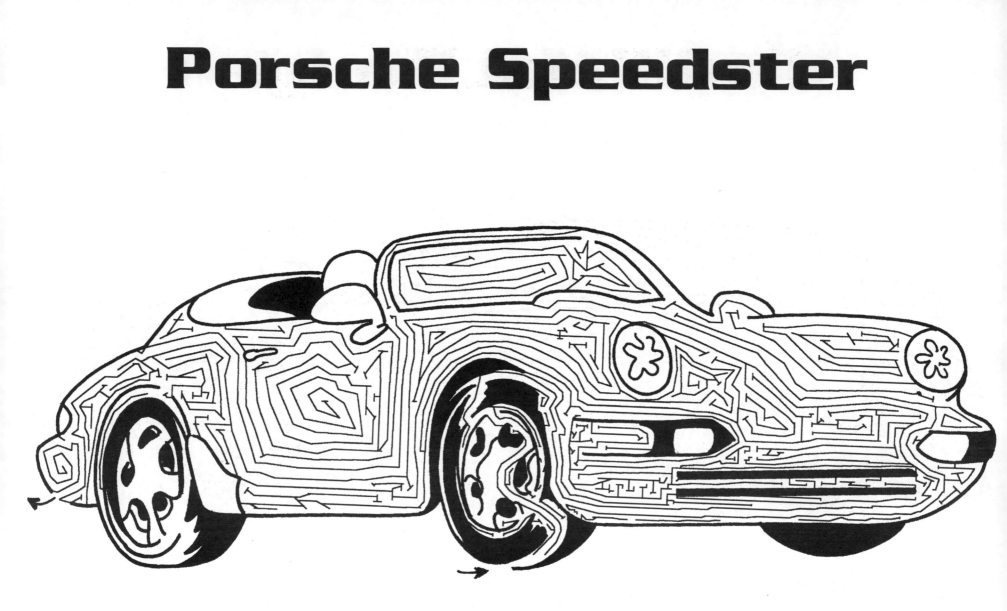

Cadillac L'Image

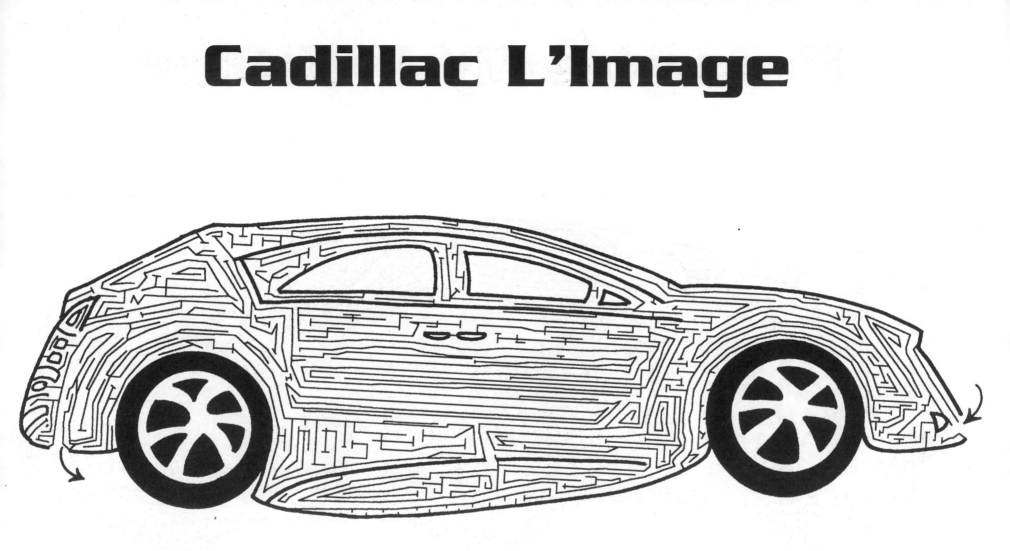

Jaguar XJ 220

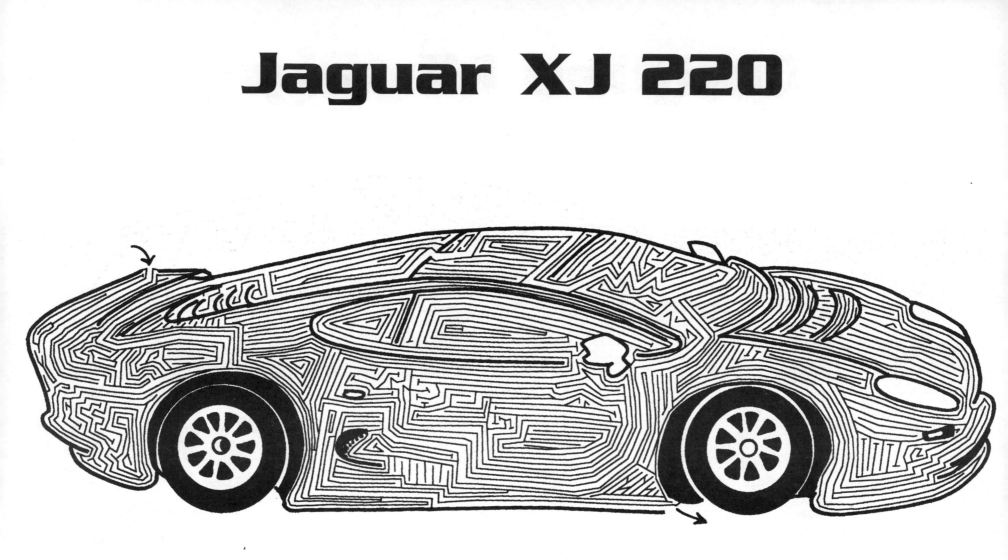

Toyota Matrix

Hyundai 2001
Concept Car

Ford Mustang

Chrysler PT Cruiser

Lotus Esprit Turbo V8

1948 Chevrolet Fleetline Aero Sedan

Pontiac Axtec GT

Buick Blackhawk

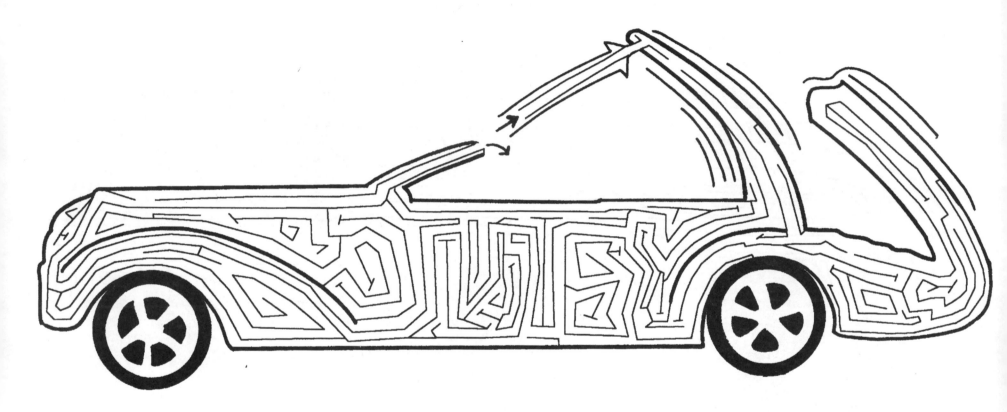

Jowett Jupiter

BMW Mini Cooper Hydrogen Car

1940 Nash Ambassador 8 Cabriolet Convertible

1998 Vision K2

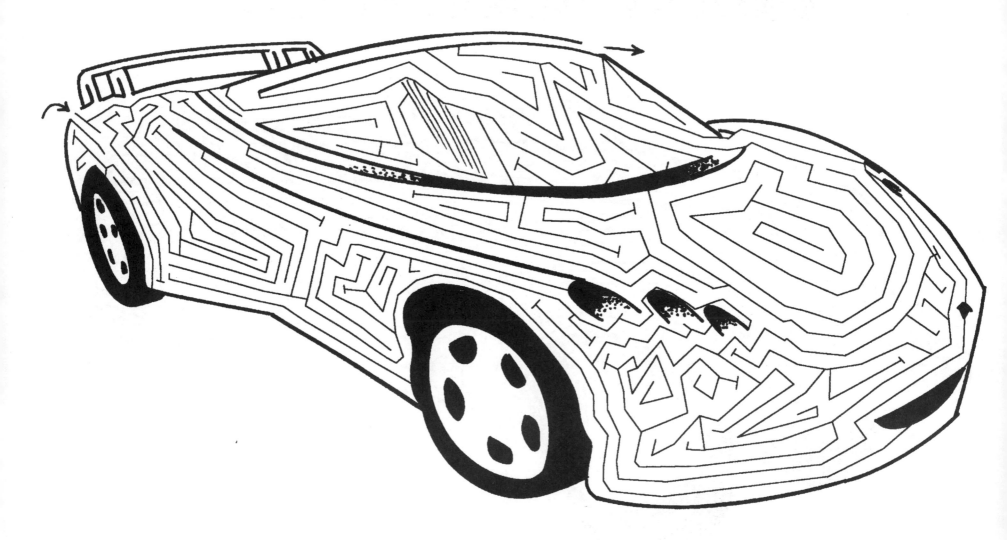

1941 Crosley Convertible Coup

1942 Packard Darrin Convertible Victoria

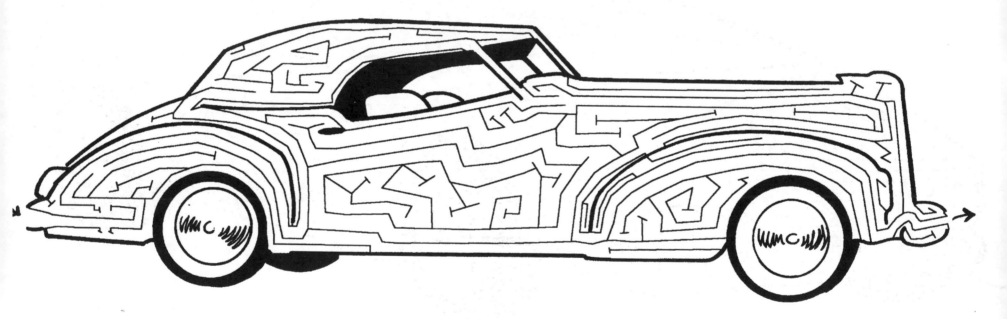

Cizetta Moroder
V-16

1949 Ferrari 166 Inter

Alpha Romeo Bat Car

Zagato Raptor

1951 Porsche 356 Cabriolet

Pontiac Banshee

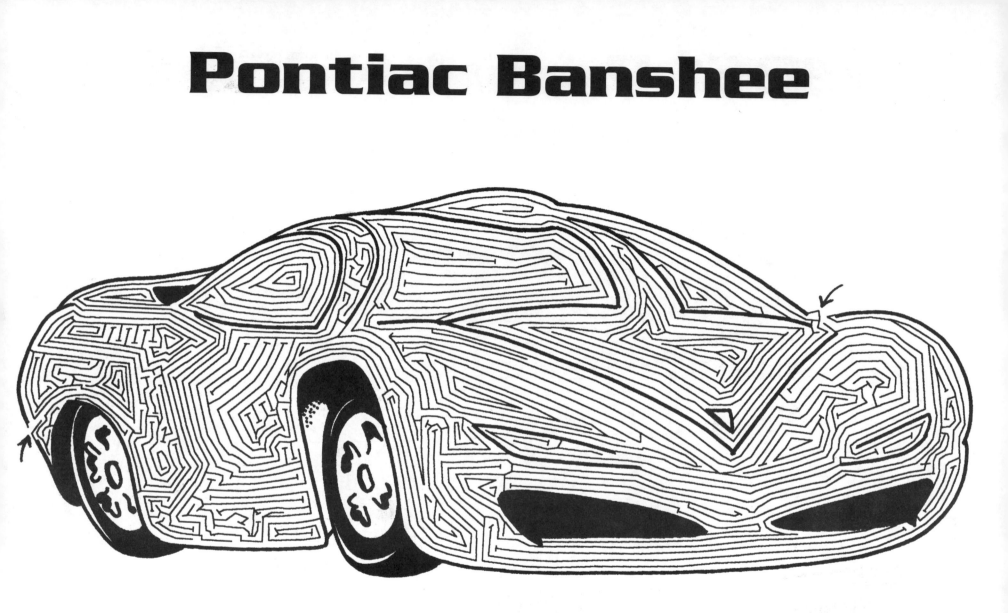

1935 Jaguar Saloon

AC Cobra

Ultima Sport

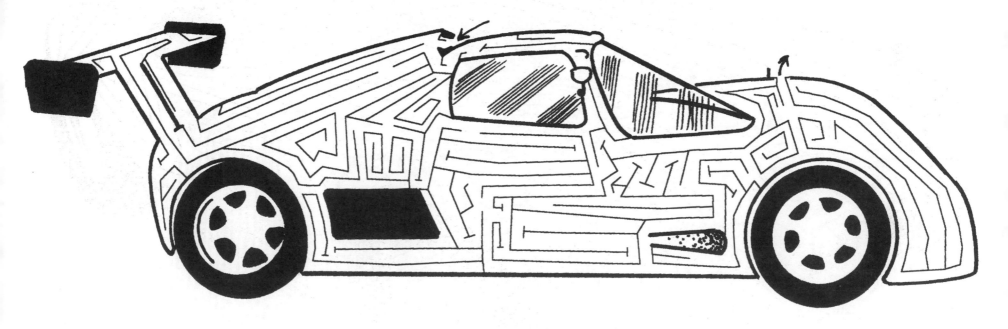

1936 Ford
Pickup Custom

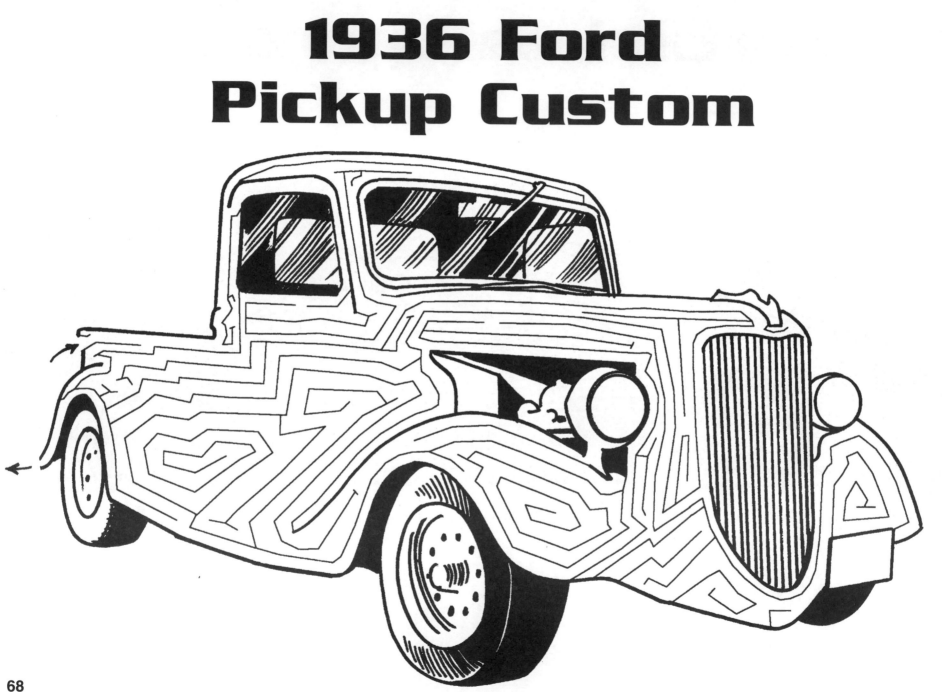

Ferrari Testarossa

1936 Plymouth 2-Door Custom

Dodge Viper

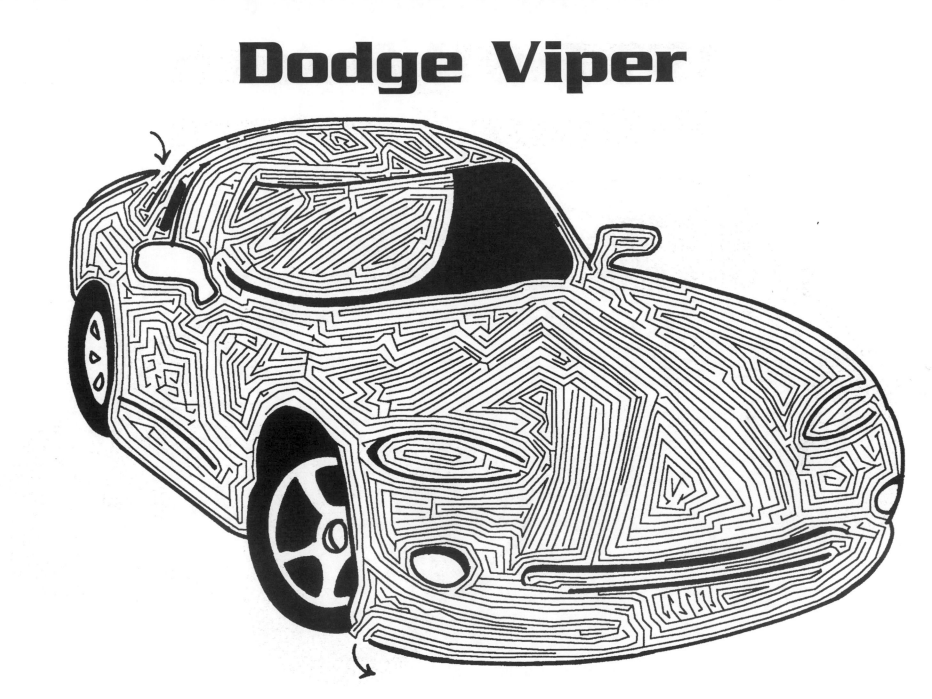

1958 Ford Fairlane

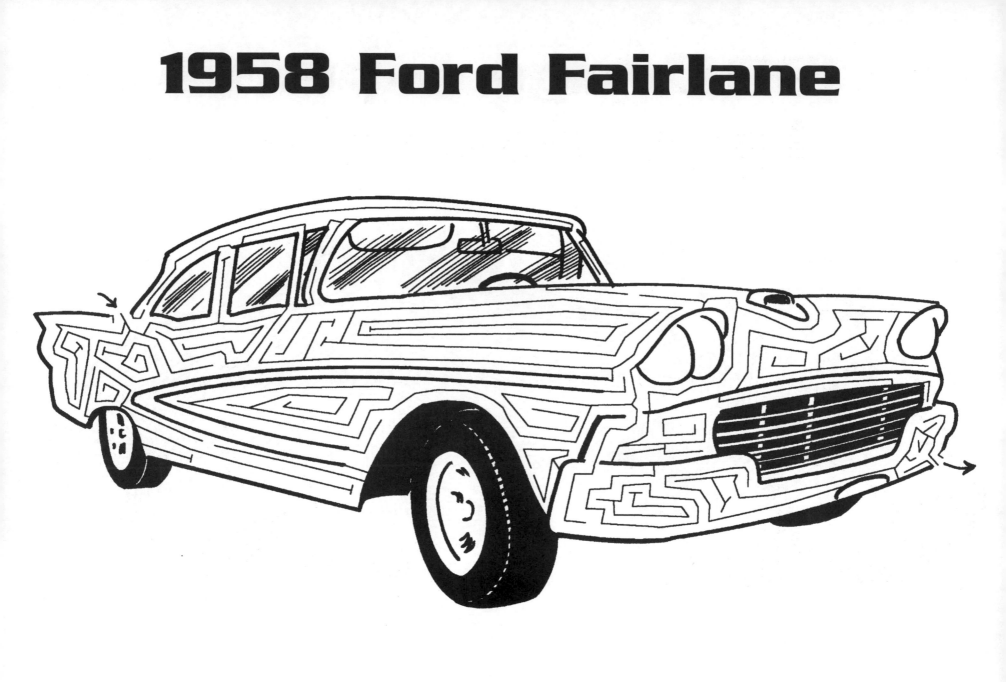

1993 Aston Martin Lagonda Vignale

Land Rover Defender

1944 Aston Martin Atom

1983 Isdera Commendatore

Cobra

Corvette Stingray

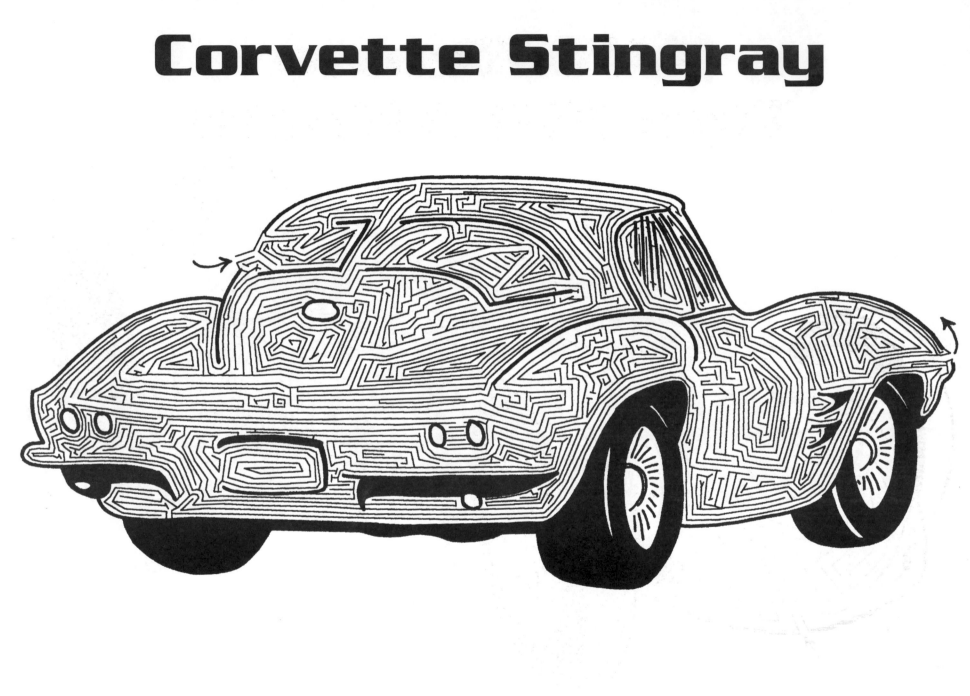

Alfa Romeo
Tipo 159 Alfetta

Volkswagon Karmann Ghia Convertible

Jaguar F Type

Porsche 911

Lamborghini Diablo

1960 Austin Healy Sprite

Monster Wheels

Answers

Page 2   **Page 3**   **Page 4**

    Page 5   **Page 6**   **Page 7**

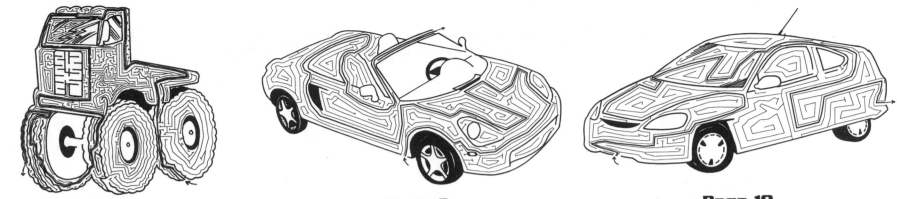

Page 8

Page 9

Page 10

Page 11

Page 12

Page 13

Page 14

Page 15

Page 16

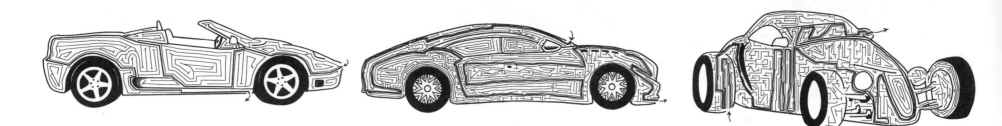

Page 17

Page 18

Page 19

Page 20

Page 21

Page 22

Page 23

Page 24

Page 25

Page 26

Page 27

Page 28

Page 29

Page 30

Page 31

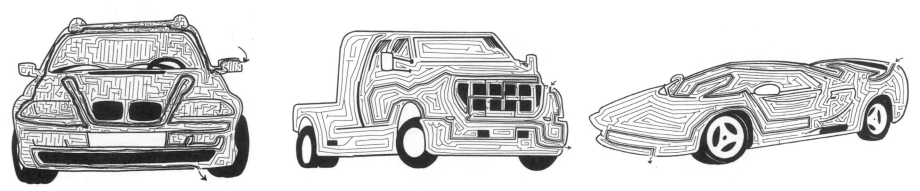

Page 32

Page 33

Page 34

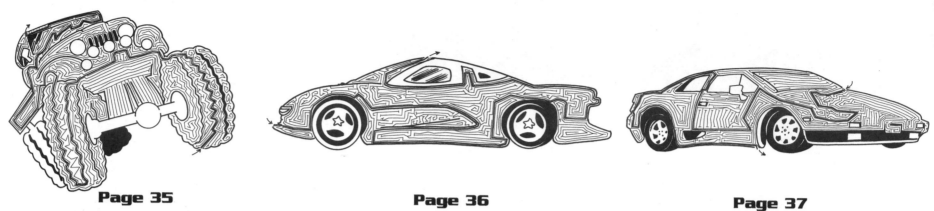

Page 35

Page 36

Page 37

Page 38

Page 39

Page 40

Page 41

Page 42

Page 43

Page 44

Page 45

Page 46

Page 47

Page 48

Page 49

Page 50

Page 51

Page 52

Page 53   **Page 54**   **Page 55**

Page 56   **Page 57**   **Page 58**

Page 59

Page 60

Page 61

Page 62

Page 63

Page 64

Page 65

Page 66

Page 67

Page 68

Page 69

Page 70

Page 71

Page 72

Page 73

Page 74

Page 75

Page 76

Page 77

Page 78

Page 79

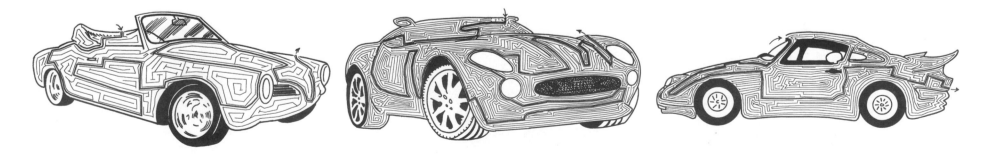

Page 80

Page 81

Page 82

Page 83

Page 84

Page 85